Kayaking WITH Eric Jackson

STROKES and CONCEPTS

Kayaking WITH Eric Jackson

STROKES and CONCEPTS

Second Edition

Eric Jackson

STACKPOLE
BOOKS

Guilford, Connecticut

Published by Stackpole Books
An imprint of Globe Pequot
Trade Division of The Rowman & Littlefield Publishing Group, Inc.
4501 Forbes Boulevard, Suite 200, Lanham, Maryland 20706

Distributed by NATIONAL BOOK NETWORK
800-462-6420

British Library Cataloguing in Publication Information available
Library of Congress Cataloging-in-Publication Data available

ISBN 978-0-8117-1835-6 (paperback)
ISBN 978-0-8117-6560-2 (e-book)

♾™ The paper used in this publication meets the minimum requirements of American National Standard for Information Sciences—Permanence of Paper for Printed Library Materials, ANSI/NISO Z39.48-1992.

Printed in the United States of America

CONTENTS

Introduction... vii

CHAPTER 1: THE 12-MINUTE STROKE DRILL WARM-UP......... 1
Getting Started.. 3
Head, Paddle, Boat, and Body............................ 3
Committing the Rules to Habit........................... 8

CHAPTER 2: THE CONCEPTS: SPEED, ANGLE, ARC,
AND SPIN-MOMENTUM 9

CHAPTER 3: FORWARD STROKE 11
The Stroke... 11

CHAPTER 4: REVERSE STROKE...................... 19
The Stroke... 19

CHAPTER 5: PRIMARY TURNING STROKES 26
The First Two Rules of Turning 27
Forward Sweep 27
Reverse Sweep.. 31

CHAPTER 6: SECONDARY TURNING STROKES 35
The Turning Force of Spin-Momentum 36
The Third Rule of Turning 37
Draw Stroke.. 37
The Fourth Rule of Turning............................. 45
Compound Strokes 46
C-Stroke... 46
S-Turn Stroke 54
Reverse Compound Stroke 62

Offside C-Stroke 70
Sideslip Stroke 74
Reverse Sweep Torso Drill 77
Squirt Stroke 78
Initiation Stroke for Playboating 81

**CHAPTER 7: APPLYING THE STROKES AND CONCEPTS
TO WHITEWATER 84**
Four Whitewater Concepts 84
Eddy Turns 85
Ferrying 91
Whitewater S-Turns 98
Surfing Holes 99
Surfing Waves 108
Boofing 109
Boofing over Holes 115

Summary 117

INTRODUCTION

Strokes and concepts for kayaking have continued to evolve over the past twenty years, mostly due to the evolution of kayaks. But despite this, your success in any kayaking endeavor will still depend upon your basic habits related to your head, paddle, boat, and body movements or non-movements. Your kayak goes where it goes based on a combination of your own physical effort and how effectively you use the river's energy. This book provides the information, drills, and coaching you need to learn, understand, and put to use the best techniques available today. I will cover both the shortest kayaks (playboats) and the longer river-running and creek boats, as there are differences.

I have seen the value of learning the kayaking basics from all of the successful racers, freestyle paddlers, and general river runners that I have coached over the years. The basic strokes and concepts are the foundation on which all other skills are built. Cultivating the best general habits for your head, paddle, boat, and body will make the incredibly complex whitewater environment much more manageable.

In the eighteen years since I wrote the first edition of *Strokes and Concepts*, I have won three more world championship freestyle titles and countless races, and I have coached my friends and family members to many more World Championship titles, successful first descents, and racing victories. Learning and applying the basics is critical for effective paddling and will increase your enjoyment of the sport.

Whether you are a beginner, thinking about trying the sport, or an aspiring pro kayaker, this book can be a valuable reference guide to paddling. Remember, "Good strokes can take you to good places!"

Learning new skills and improving existing ones is very rewarding.

CHAPTER 1

The 12-Minute Stroke Drill Warm-Up

The best place to create the good habits for whitewater is in flatwater. Flatwater is a controlled environment where you can focus on one thing at a time and coach yourself.

When you are paddling in whitewater, you tend to focus on the rapids and the moves you are doing, but you will still be relying on the basic techniques. If you haven't learned all these techniques carefully, the chance of

Flatwater gives you time to focus on your skills without the distractions of whitewater.

your strokes being ideal is slim. The best paddlers seem to be able to paddle almost effortlessly; their strokes and concepts work for them even when they are not actively thinking about them. This book is designed to teach you how to do that for yourself.

Each chapter of this book will teach you a stroke, teach you a skill, or introduce you to some concepts you can apply to your paddling. When you've practiced the effective techniques for each stroke so much that they become habit, you'll experience a breakthrough in paddling. You will be able to learn new things easily in playboating, river running, racing, and more. The biggest obstacle you'll have to overcome in learning new skills is how to properly control your head, paddle, boat, and body at the same time but independently. If your habits for your head are not correct or if your habits for your torso are not correct, your paddle and boat control will not be correct, and you will have a difficult time learning new skills.

The concept of the 12-Minute Stroke Drill Warm-Up is to practice all of the strokes when you first get on the water. Once you have committed the strokes to memory and can use your head, paddle, boat, and body to achieve the desired effect, you are on your way to creating good habits. If you can remember the lessons I am teaching here and focus on fixing what you're doing wrong, you will keep a constant progression.

One of my favorite sayings is "Everyone rises to their own level of incompetence and then remains there." This is especially true for kayaking. The moment you think you are doing the strokes perfectly is the moment you stop improving.

Whitewater uses up your random access memory.

I have to focus on my strokes every time I paddle to improve them. My forward stroke can slip easily if I don't treat it like I am learning it for the first time whenever I get in the water and warm up properly.

So, please, take the time to practice each stroke, record yourself on video doing them, and compare your results to the photos in this book or to the videos in my *Strokes and Concepts* DVD. Become a student of the sport. It is fun and rewarding, and you'll be surprised at how quickly your paddling improves. Without thinking about it, you will begin applying the skills you've been practicing in flatwater but couldn't imagine using in whitewater.

Getting Started

Unless you have done drills specifically designed to help you control your head, paddle, boat, and body, you have some specific limitations.

Here are the standard issues that 99 percent of kayakers have. Without recognizing them and learning how to replace them with proper habits, those kayakers will never overcome.

1. **Your head is stuck to your torso.** This means that you don't freely move your head around and look at your target. Instead, your default head position is straight ahead over your bow. It is going to take some practice to break free of this habit.
2. **Your torso is stuck to your hips.** You don't rotate at the waist, but you have your torso locked in the forward position as well. This is obvious in the forward stroke and your turning strokes. Fixing this is the first step to improving your stroke.
3. **Your paddle usage isn't optimized.** Your blade angles are not correct, and sometimes you paddle in the wrong direction. Understanding blade angles and when to use what strokes will get you much farther faster and in better control.
4. **Your boat angles are not being controlled, or lots of random edges are being dropped.** This makes it more difficult to keep your boat under control. We'll learn how to fix that, too.

Head, Paddle, Boat, and Body

In kayaking you have the four things to control, all at the same time, but all independently: your head, your paddle, your boat, and your body. Each of these things has specific rules you need to follow or actions you need to perform that will help you succeed in the task at hand—whether it's a roll, an airscrew, a sweep stroke, or a boof. Understanding what you are supposed to do with your head, paddle, boat, and body is step one. Knowing a drill to help you train your body in a comfortable situation helps create the muscle memory you need to allow you to focus on one important thing, while the other three things fall into place automatically. After you can control the boat with

When you peel out of an eddy, you should rarely have to think about your head, paddle, boat, and body. Developing the right habits is key to having good strokes.

your own body movements, you still have the many challenges and variables that whitewater brings when running a rapid, playing, or racing. Committing your most basic boat control skills to habit opens your brain up to focus on the whitewater.

Some basic rules for each for different paddling situations:

Head: Your head should look in the direction you want to go.

1. When upright and paddling, you should look at the target you're heading toward, point your nose at it, and stay on it until you get there.
2. When upside down, your head should look where you want your paddle and body to go, following your paddle blade (the power blade doing the work) during the roll.
3. When playboating and cartwheeling or spinning on a hole or wave, your head should still look at its target, which is where you want the end of your kayak to go next into the hole or wave.

Paddle: Your paddle should push or pull you in the direction you want to go. It's a simple concept, but it's difficult to implement in many situations. If you want to be efficient when paddling, this is the place to start.

1. Blade angle is the part of the equation that many kayakers neglect. When you take a stroke of any kind, the effectiveness of the stroke is related to the blade angle. For example, if you reach way forward to do the catch on a forward stroke and your paddle enters the water at a 45-degree angle, you only get half of the force you put into the stroke for pulling the boat

Head spotting your next target is as simple as turning, looking, and then going there.

forward. This means that if you do a 50-pound stroke, only 25 pounds is propelling you forward and 25 pounds is lifting your bow up.

2. Take strokes that actually propel you your toward your target, not away from it. For example, if I were to put you up against a group of other kayakers in a starting line in flatwater and you were the only kayaker facing backwards, 90 percent of the people will start the race with a forward sweep to turn their kayak. Only 10 percent of the people will start with a back sweep,

The paddle blade drives you toward your target.

which gets the boat moving toward the target—the finish line. The 90 percent will move about 2 feet in the wrong direction, while the 10 percent will move 2 feet in the right direction. The 10 percent will have momentum going the right way and be moving faster on their next stroke, which will be a forward sweep (since the paddle blade can push in the direction of the target once the boat has rotated over 90 degrees). By the time they do their first forward stroke (their third stroke overall), they are a good boat length or more ahead of the 90 percent who started with a forward sweep. This happens in the river all of the time. It is very common for paddlers who get turned around away from their target in a rapid, usually an eddy they want to catch, to do a forward stroke away from the eddy-line first, and then start paddling toward the eddy. This is how you can miss a hard-to-catch eddy. Knowing your target and stroking toward it is the key.

Boat: Your boat has so many different tasks depending on the situation that there are no all-encompassing rules that apply. However, there are some general guidelines that you can use for the following common situations.

1. *Rolling:* Your boat rotates upright before your body moves.
2. *General river running:* Keep your hips relaxed, and allow your boat to follow the water and waves. This allows you to keep your body upright even when going over waves and rocks. If you have a stiff lower body and try to hold the boat steady, those same waves and rocks, instead of just rocking the boat, will rock your body to the side as well, potentially tipping you over.
3. *Peel outs and eddy outs:* Edge your boat to the inside of the turn, like when you are leaning into the turn on a bike.
4. *Boat angles:* Your boat will always be turning. To move efficiently, plan your turns so that they are smooth arcs that will allow you to predict where you are going next.

Your hips control your boat edging, and your bow rarely points at your target.

Body: Your body (torso) has two main rules that apply almost 100 percent of the time. The only exceptions are in freestyle (when you are upside down and desire to be).

1. Keep your body weight quiet and over the boat. This means that you must keep your body still as much as possible, with no big forward and backward or side to side movements. A quiet upper body makes it easier to

Leading with your body and keeping it over the boat is one of the most important habits you can develop.

stay upright and easier to control your boat. You can spend your energy moving the boat where you want to go instead of using it for bracing.

2. Lead every turn with your body. The basic rule here is that if you are turning left, your body should face over the left side of the boat throughout the turn. About 90 percent of paddlers break this rule and hit a "wall" with their skill set. Leading with your body is more effective and efficient, and it makes it easier to see where you are going.

Committing the Rules to Habit

If you learn the focus for each stroke and how to coach yourself, just doing the 12-Minute Stroke Drill Warm-Up each time you get on the water will be enough to develop good habits and overcome bad ones. That is the beauty of the program—you can warm yourself up physically and learn the skills at the same time.

CHAPTER 2

The Concepts: Speed, Angle, Arc, and Spin-Momentum

Knowing four basic concepts and how they affect where your boat goes will allow you to begin applying the right strokes at the right time.

Speed: Just like the name suggests, speed is how fast your kayak is moving through the water, either forward or backward. The reason speed is such an important concept in your paddling is that it greatly affects how your kayak will act when it crosses an eddy line, and it determines how much spin-momentum you have.

Where your boat goes in whitewater has to do with speed, angle, arc, and spin-momentum.

Angle: The angle at which your kayak crosses an eddy-line or current differential is essential. It also determines how the eddy-line affects your kayak when you cross it.

Arc: The spinning motion your kayak should make when you cross an eddy-line or maneuver your kayak through a rapid is called the arc. A smooth arc is the most efficient and allows you to harness spin-momentum and the river's energy.

Spin-momentum: Spin-momentum is a force that your kayak has when you paddle forward or backward. It comes from the way a kayak creates a bow wave and then tries to climb its own wave. Essentially, a whitewater kayak is always paddling uphill, and the bow is always trying to fall off of the wave to one side or another. The force of the bow trying to fall off of the wave is spin-momentum. A beginner struggles to paddle straight for very long without spinning out due to spin-momentum. What most kayakers don't understand is that you can't paddle a kayak straight. You can only string together a series of left and right turns in a way that gets you where you want to go in what appears to be a straight line. To test this out for yourself, paddle your kayak forward as straight as you can, then take your paddle out of the water and coast until you stop. You will always spin out to the left or the right and end up backward. Which way will you spin? The way you are already spinning when you stopped. In theory, if you were perfectly straight and there was no wind or body movements, you might be able to coast to a stop without spinning, but I have never seen it happen or been able to do it myself. Learning to harness spin-momentum is an important part of learning to paddle efficiently and work with your kayak, not against it.

In the following chapters, you will learn how to apply these concepts in whitewater and how to use speed, arc, and spin-momentum in flatwater during stroke drills.

CHAPTER 3

Forward Stroke

The forward stroke is one of the most important strokes for learning to separate your head, paddle, boat, and body and beginning to have control over them for all situations. It will be your workhorse stroke for getting from Point A to Point B.

DRILL

100 forward strokes
50 slow, 25 medium, 25 fast

The Stroke

HEAD

- Point your head at your target, which is most likely going to be straight in front of you. This is easiest when you're not yet using torso rotation in your forward stroke. Once you begin adding torso rotation, you'll find that your head wants to rotate back and forth with your torso. At that stage, you'll need to focus on your head again.

PADDLE

- Your paddle should go in the water at your toes, and come out of the water at your butt.
- The paddle should be as vertical as possible from both the side view and the front view. The more vertical the paddle is in the front view, the closer the blade is to the center line of the kayak, and it will pull you forward

11

more efficiently. The further the blade is from the center line (and the less vertical you hold the paddle), the more the paddle turns the boat on each stroke and the less it pulls the boat forward.

- The more vertical the paddle is during the stroke in the side view, the more effectively you can pull the boat forward also. If the paddle is vertical and you put 40 pounds of force on it, you will be pulling the boat with 40 pounds of force. If the paddle goes in at a 45-degree angle (for example, if your top hand is back by your face and your bottom hand is extended), then only 20 pounds out of the 40 will be pulling you forward and the other 20 pounds will be lifting your bow up. The efficiency of your forward stroke depends on your blade angle, and your top hand is in charge of setting your blade angle. To get a vertical stroke throughout, you'll need to start with your top arm partially extended and finish the stroke with the top hand not fully extended.

BOAT

- When doing the forward stroke, your goal is to keep the boat flat. Avoid side to side rocking (edge dropping). This will be easy if you are not using any torso rotation, which you most likely are not. Once you begin using torso rotation, you must separate the movement of your torso from your hips. This takes practice.
- Your boat will yaw back and forth with each stroke. Your goal is to keep the yaw to a minimum. The shorter the boat, the more the yaw will be. To keep the yaw to a minimum, keep the paddle blade close to the boat with a vertical paddle.

BODY

- Your body should be quiet and not lunging forward or backward during the strokes. Don't "reach" with your body by leaning more forward, and don't pull back on the paddle by leaning back
- Torso rotation will be a theme for the rest of this book, and if there's one thing you need to know, it's that you probably don't have any torso rotation in your forward stroke, even if you think you do. I know it sounds presumptuous, but this has been my experience from watching and teaching many thousands of kayakers of all skill levels. Those who do have some torso rotation usually only have about 50 percent of the desired amount.
- Try sitting in your chair or kayak and looking down at your chest, and then extend your right arm in front of you. Now rotate your body to the left by twisting at the waist. Pin your left shoulder backward and push your right shoulder and arm forward as far as you can. This is torso rotation. You are now "wound up." Now pull your arm and right shoulder as far back as you can, pushing your left shoulder forward. You just "unwound" and then wound up the other way. Your forward stroke is strongest when you begin the stroke wound up like a spring.

Finish forward stroke with angled paddle.

Finish forward stroke with vertical paddle.

- Also, the speed at which you can pull yourself forward is the speed of your arms pulling the paddle back combined with the speed of your torso pulling the paddle back. Your top end speed is greater with torso rotation, and it also will give you a longer stroke with a more vertical paddle.

Catch at eye level, blade at toes, body wound up, head straight, boat flat.

End of the stroke—body wound up, head straight, blade at hip, boat flat, ready for next stroke.

- To determine if you are rotating your torso when you are paddling forward, look at your life jacket. It should be rotating back and forth against your spray skirt, about 45 degrees each way.

- Do not look at your arms swinging in front of your face as an indicator of torso rotation, as it will fake you out.

Now, put it all together to make a good forward stroke for the first time:

1. Start with your paddle position. Very, very slowly put your right paddle blade in at your toes, with your left hand just left of and in front of your left eye. Pull your right blade back slowly until it reaches your butt. Take the right blade out and try the left blade. Right now, your only focus should be paddle position. Try to keep the blade as vertical as possible from the side view as you can. Avoid punching the top hand all of the way out or having the top hand too far back at the beginning of the stroke.

2. Now look at your life jacket and notice whether it is moving 45 degrees back and forth like you want. If it isn't, stop paddling immediately, wind up your body, and then put your paddle in and unwind. Switch sides and repeat. If you don't do this slowly and deliberately, you will not be able to make your torso cooperate. If you just start paddling along, you will not learn anything, you will not get your torso moving, and this drill and the others will not achieve their primary goal—to teach you how to control your head, paddle, boat, and body all separately but at the same time. If you are already using some torso (maybe 5 percent of the readers will be doing this), try to use more, going for as much as your body will allow.

Focus on max torso paddle at toes, head straight, boat flat, and ready for a slow stroke to get things going.

3. Once you get some torso rotation going, it is time to see if you are keeping your head straight, or if it is moving with your torso, instead of independently. Most of the time, as soon as I ask students to try to hold their head still, they can, but they stop using their torso. If I ask them to start using their torso again, they start moving their head. The trick to knowing if your head is still is to close one eye and put your nose over the bow of the boat. See if your nose stays over the bow or if it swings back and forth.

4. Finally, if you are able to keep your head straight, rotate your torso, and use the correct paddle motion, check to see whether your boat is staying flat or whether you are rocking it back and forth on each stroke. Typically, when somebody is learning to use the torso, they lean the boat toward the stroke, because separating your torso rotation and hips for edge control takes practice. You can actually develop good edge control just by learning a good forward stroke!

FORWARD STROKE REVIEW

1. **Level 1: Learning.** Start off in super slow motion, really focusing on the paddle placement, then the torso rotation, then keeping your head straight, and then keeping the boat flat in the first 20 strokes. Slowly pick up the speed until you are paddling at a normal pace by 50 strokes. Increase to a medium pace for the next 25 strokes, double-checking your torso rotation every 10 strokes or so. Finish with 25 above-average-paced strokes—it's important to begin trying different paces so that your stroke won't fall apart at faster speeds.

2. **Level 2: Getting Proficient.** Now you should be able to use torso rotation without thinking too much about it. You can keep your boat flat, your head straight, and your paddle nice and vertical. The next step is to improve your efficiency with better stroke and torso timing. Your boat slows down in between each stroke. To maintain a certain speed, you have to accelerate your boat to go faster than your desired speed on each stroke so that when it decelerates in between strokes, you are averaging the speed you want. If you want to improve your speed and efficiency, you need to reduce the break time in between strokes. To do this, consciously drop your next stroke immediately after the previous one is finished. Think about the switch from one stroke to the next as being almost without any pause. The other benefit of this focus is that if you do have a short pause in between strokes, you are likely to unwind in between strokes, and you won't get the benefit of the spring action in your body. You should feel like a gear in motion, with a constant amount of blade pressure at all times—you shouldn't feel as if you're caught in a cycle of pull, glide, pull, glide. The amount of force you need for each stroke will be less because you don't have to re-accelerate each time. In fact, for example,

depending on just how well you do it, you can reduce the amount of force required to paddle 6 miles per hour from 40-pound strokes to 25-pound strokes. This reduces fatigue and will make your stroke feel more like endurance-pace paddling instead of sprinting.

- **Drill:** Start off with a speed just below your normal speed for the first 25 strokes, and then slowly pick up the pace strokes 25 to 50, really focusing on maintaining a fluid stroke, quick turnover between strokes, and good torso rotation. For strokes 50 to 75, speed up to a fast endurance pace (but not sprinting) and try to maintain a good stroke at this pace. Finish the drill with strokes 75 to 100 at close to a full sprint, again really trying to hold your technique together in spite of the faster pace and your fatigue. You will be tempted to shorten your stroke to do a faster stroke rate, but instead keep the stroke long, keep the torso doing much of the work, stay fully wound up, and keep the paddle vertical.

3. **Level 3: Whitewater Warm-Up.** Once you are proficient with the forward stroke in flat water, it usually takes about 10,000 strokes of focused practice and paying attention to have your flatwater forward stroke before you become proficient and establish good habits. Get somebody to record your stroke on video occasionally to be sure that you're doing what you think you are. Assuming you are on the right track, you can begin to warm up in whitewater and practice your stroke while doing ferries or running down rapids.

Learning to use good technique when sprinting will improve your paddling when it really matters, like getting on a wave that is hard to catch.

- **Drill:** Do 50 slow strokes, 25 medium strokes, and 25 fast strokes, but this time in whitewater. Focus on stroke timing, working with the water and placing your strokes so that you keep your bow dry when going down through waves, as well as timing in and out of eddies. Ferries are always a good warm-up, and you'll have to deal with boils, waves, and eddy-lines. Continue to check your torso rotation, as this is the hardest thing to learn. Good torso rotation is a habit you need for whitewater.

CHAPTER 4

Reverse Stroke

Your kayak is designed to go backward and forward, so you need to learn to go backward too. Back ferries, boat scouting, and backing away from obstacles are all easier if you are comfortable going backward.

DRILL

60 backstrokes
30 slow, 15 medium, 15 fast

The Stroke

Head: Your head should look over your shoulder every few strokes. Pick a side that gives you the best view of where you are going and look over that shoulder at least once every 5 strokes.

Paddle: Your paddle should go in at your butt and out at your toes. The top hand's job is to make the paddle as vertical as it can comfortably go. Most people do back sweeps in order to paddle backward, paddling low to the water with both hands. Getting the top hand up to create a more vertical paddle will give you more speed. With the top hand up, the position you are in is not as strong as when you keep your hands low, but the effect each stroke has will be greater.

Boat: If you are in a river runner or creek boat, keep the boat flat, with no edge, trying not to rock the boat back and forth.

Body: Keep your weight forward, especially in a playboat, as the stern will go under if you don't. Use your torso on the reverse stroke as well. Watch your life jacket again, as you did with the forward stroke, to monitor how much torso you are using. The goal is for the life jacket to move 45 degrees in each direction.

Plant backstroke.

Finish of backstroke.

Paddling backward is challenging at first, and just trying to stay straight without any real correction strokes is difficult. The reason is spin-momentum and lack of awareness of where you are. You learned to paddle forward in a straight line pretty quickly, and eventually, you'll learn to paddle backward in a straight line quickly. If you are not able to easily paddle backward yet without turning, you are not practicing it enough to consider it a functional skill to use on the river. This drill will quickly increase your awareness of where you are when you're moving backward. Your head, paddle, boat, and body will come together quite easily as most people find it easier to use their torso when moving backward than when moving forward.

Use torso rotation getting paddle in a hip.

Full torso rotation and paddle out at toes.

Look over your shoulder every few strokes to see where you are going.

Keeping weight forward helps keep the stern out of the water on playboats.

REVERSE STROKE REVIEW

Level 1 Drill: Start off very slowly, looking over your shoulder every few strokes and trying to avoid spinning out. By the time you are at 30 strokes, pick up the speed to a medium pace. From strokes 30 to 45, continue going

Reverse stroke looking.

Reverse stroke moving.

at a medium pace, focusing on torso and paddle position. From strokes 45 to 60, focus on holding on and not quitting, as well as keeping your technique together. You will feel a burning in your shoulders from this drill. This burning feeling is the blood pumping into your shoulders and warming those muscles up. You will also be surprised at how quickly you get stronger going backward both physically and technically.

Level 2 Drill: Start off at a medium pace for 30 strokes, increasing to fast at 30 and then sprinting at 45.

Level 3 Drill: Practice the same skills, but in whitewater. Try back ferries, back peel outs, and running downstream backward (where you know the river and know there are not any dangers in the way).

Planting a reverse stroke to slow down and begin a turn on Big Timber Creek in Montana.

CHAPTER 5

Primary Turning Strokes

Primary turning strokes are the strokes you use to get the boat spinning in the right direction. They are your strongest turning strokes. Because you'll now be learning how to turn the kayak, you need to learn a few new rules that will make a big difference in your boating.

The First Two Rules of Turning

YOUR HEAD ALWAYS LOOKS AT YOUR TARGET

I mentioned this rule in a previous chapter, but if you're following along, chances are, you still haven't mastered it yet. In order to have your head look at your target, you need to know what your target is and spot that target no matter where your boat is pointed. Most people can look at their target only if the boat is pointed at the target. On a peel out, during a ferry, or during most moves that require turning, the bow of the boat is not pointed where you are going. However, your head should be.

YOUR BODY SHOULD LEAD EVERY TURN

If you want your boat to turn to the left, you should first turn your body to the left, pointing your chest over the left side of the boat. Keep your body pointed over the left side of the boat until you are done turning or until you want to turn the other way. What's cool about this rule is just how universal it is. Remember how the forward stroke is a turning stroke, since it makes the kayak turn left and right on each stroke in order for the the kayak to go straight overall? You use torso during your forward stroke for the same reason that you use your body to lead a turn. When you are wound-up for a right stroke, your body is pointing over the left side of the boat, preparing for your right stroke, which will make the boat turn left. The most common mistake people make when turning is to let their body get behind the turn, which has devastating effects on your turning ability, overall control of the boat, speed, ability to see, and for a playboater, your ability to do moves.

Forward Sweep

DRILL

10 forward sweeps on the left
10 forward sweeps on the right

Use the forward sweep when you want to move the boat forward and get it turning at the same time. A forward sweep in its pure form is most effective for turning, or you can make a stroke that falls somewhere between a forward sweep and a forward stroke for situations when you don't need as much turning force.

Head: Point your head at your target. For this drill, you will be going in circles—imagine a dog chasing its tail—so you will never get to your target. Your target will be the stern of your kayak.

Body: Start off with your body rotated in the direction you plan on turning, and then remain there until you are doing sweeps. If you are turning left, rotate your body left and keep it fully wound up throughout the sweep. You have most likely been taught to unwind or use torso in your sweep, but you shouldn't do that now.

Boat: Keep the boat flat for this drill, and try not to use any edge during the sweep.

Forward sweep start.

Forward sweep middle.

Paddle: As with the forward stroke, the paddle should go in at your toes and out at your hip, but in this case, the top hand should be as far back and low as possible. The goal is to position the paddle to push the bow straight away from the blade. Remember that every paddle stroke should push you in the direction you want to go. You want the bow to push straight to the side to rotate the boat as quickly as possible.

Forward sweep finish.

Forward sweep.

If you want to keep turning when you do a forward sweep, the reason why you shouldn't unwind or use your torso is because if you keep your body wound up, your sweep will rotate your body weight as well as your kayak, and the mass of your body will help carry the boat around the turn after you finish the sweep. When you unwind or use torso in the sweep, your body is actually stationary along with the paddle in the water and only the boat and your legs get moving from the sweep. Because of the way water resistance works (it becomes eight times stronger when you move your boat twice as fast), using torso causes most of the energy you used in the sweep to bleed away in the form of water resistance. Add to that the fact that your body weight isn't moving and the boat's momentum now has to get your body moving at the end of the sweep and you don't get as far on a single sweep. The drill I do shows how you can do a proper sweep, keeping your body leading the turn and with only two sweeps so that you can make a full 360-degree turn with lots of extra speed at the end. It takes three sweeps to do the same thing using a much longer, full-torso sweep that was traditionally taught in kayak schools and certification classes (meaning that you have to learn how to do the sweep incorrectly to be able to teach kayaking in most countries).

Bad forward sweep.

FORWARD SWEEP REVIEW

Level 1 Drill: During the sweep, keep your eyes focused on your stern, and keep the boat flat.

Level 2 Drill: Pick a piece of water that you are sweeping to as your target, and keep finding and quickly focusing on your piece of water. This gives you practice picking and focusing on targets quickly.

Level 3 Drill: Using a playboat, practice dropping your outside edge and sweeping your stern under the water, with your bow up in the air. This drill is a combination of edge control and lifting your knees to engage the stern at the right moment.

Reverse Sweep

DRILL

10 reverse sweeps on the left
10 reverse sweeps on the right

Head: Again, your head should look at your target, which in this case, is the stern. Lead with your head—don't follow! Many people look where they were instead of where they are going, but if you are turning left, then you should turn your head to the left.

Body: Again, lead the turns with your body. To do a left reverse sweep, rotate your body as far to the left as you can and keep it rotated left throughout.

Boat: Keep the boat flat for the drills.

Paddle: As with the forward sweep, you want to get as much turning force from the stroke as possible. Reach your left hand as far back as you can with a straight back arm. If you have a playboat, reach behind the stern. Your right arm should reach across the deck to make the paddle parallel to the boat again so that you are pushing the stern straight away from the paddle blade.

Reverse sweep start.

Reverse sweep finish.

Reverse sweep reaching.

Reverse sweep.

REVERSE SWEEP REVIEW

Level 1 Drill: Do 10 sweeps on each side, nice and slow, watching to make sure your back arm is straight and as far back as it can reach. Keep your boat flat.

Level 2 Drill: Combine your forward and reverse sweeps, alternating between them. Spin in one direction, and then, after you have done 10 of each one way, repeat in the other direction.

Level 3 Drill: Practice dropping your outside edge on a playboat and squirting the stern under the water. Lifting on your knees will help a lot.

CHAPTER 6

Secondary Turning Strokes

M astering secondary turning strokes will teach you how to paddle more efficiently when turning, harness spin-momentum, and learn paddle dexterity.

The Turning Force of Spin-Momentum

Remember that you always, always have spin-momentum in one direciton or another. Harnessing it is not difficult, but you need to be aware of it and learn the strokes that will put it to work for you. The general concept is that when you paddle forward, your boat naturally wants to start turning one way or another. Instead of paddling randomly and hoping that spin-momentum goes in the direction you want it to, you can paddle deliberately in a way that makes the boat always turn the right way. Once you begin doing that, you can predict where your boat is going to go much better, and you can use the secondary turning strokes you're about to learn to control those turns and actually harness both your spin-momentum and the force of the river itself.

YOUR FIRST SPIN-MOMENTUM DRILL

Paddle your boat forward to get up to a fast pace, get it spinning to the right, and immediately begin paddling only on the right side, with no left strokes. If you do it correctly, you'll find that you can go in a right-hand circle indefinitely. The keys to continuing to turn right while paddling on the right side are:

1. *Paddle close to the boat.* Don't sweep the boat to the left!! A vertical paddle with the blade as close to the boat as possible will provide as much forward momentum as possible without overpowering your spin-momentum.

2. *Keep the speed up.* Remember that how much spin-momentum you have is based on how fast you are going. If you're barely moving, you won't have much spin-momentum, and any forward strokes will overpower it, causing you to start spinning left.

Try this drill on the left side as well.

Vertical paddle spin-momentum.

The Third Rule of Turning

This drill should help you learn that you can paddle on the right side of the boat only and the boat can keep turning right, as long as your paddle strokes don't overpower the spin-momentum. Realizing this is the first step to harnessing spin-momentum. If you were to try a drill where you paddle on both sides of the boat in a circle, or just on the inside of the turn, you would find that you can go around a turn faster on just the inside and with much less energy. The reason for this is that stroking on the inside of the turn keeps the boat from sliding as much and losing its forward momentum. This brings us to an important rule for turning your kayak:

Always paddle on the inside of the turn.

Draw Stroke

The next stroke you are going to learn is a game changer: the draw stroke. What is special about the draw stroke is that (when done properly), it allows your paddle to act like a keel and a sail for the kayak. Without the draw stroke, you can only pull yourself forward, push backward, and spin. With the draw stroke, you can carry your speed around turns, harness the current differentials in the river, and control the boat much more effectively.

Your whitewater kayak doesn't carve a turn very well. It is designed to slide on turns and be very maneuverable. The shorter the kayak, the less it carves and the more it slides. Imagine having a racecar out on a frozen lake and trying to run through a course. It would just slide around, and you would not make any good turns. This is the whitewater kayak without a draw stroke. What a kayak needs to carve around turns is a sort of "keel." On a sailboat, the keel prevents the boat from sliding sideways. The role of the draw stroke is to mimic a keel, preventing the boat from sliding to the outside of the turn.

Where does a keel go on a boat? Unfortunately for kayakers, it has been taught for decades that you should put your draw stroke in at the bow of the boat and use it to turn the kayak. But if you were to put a keel on a sailboat at the bow, the sail boat would not sail—it would just turn into the wind and sit there. The same is true for a kayak: if the draw stroke goes in at the bow, the stern just slides out and you stop, just as if you didn't put a stroke in at all. The draw stroke needs to keep the stern from sliding out, so it should go just behind your center of buoyancy (your butt).

Head: Look to your target on the inside of the turn.

Boat: Keep your boat flat.

Body: Lead the turn with your body (face the inside of the turn), and keep it over the boat.

Paddle: Keep a vertical paddle parallel to the boat, with the power face toward the boat and the blade behind the butt.

Here is how you do that:

THE DRAW

- Take your paddle and hold it in your right hand only.
- Put the paddle vertically into the water next to your butt on the right side.
- Now turn the face of the blade so that the power face is facing your kayak, making it so the paddle would slice or feather along the length of the boat.

Normal draw paddle position.

- After that, turn your body to face the paddle shaft, and then reach your left hand over and grab the paddle. You are now in the "normal draw" position.
- Move the paddle farther back to your stern—this is a stern draw with a normal face.
- Move the paddle to the right knee—this is a bow draw with a normal face.
- Now rotate the leading edge of the paddle (the edge closer to your bow) toward the boat by 30 degrees. This is a closed-face bow draw.
- Rotate the leading edge away from the boat. This is an open-face bow draw.
- By now you have mastered all the different combinations: bow, normal, or stern draw and open, closed, or normal face.

Normal-face bow draw paddle position.

Closed-face bow draw.

Open-face bow draw.

DRAW STROKE REVIEW

Drill 1: Paddle forward, and get some good speed. Get the boat spinning to the right, and then before you let the boat spin out and slide, throw your normal-face stern draw in the water.
- If you hit it right, you'll carve a long, steady turn and won't slide a bit.
- If you put the draw in too far forward (because that is your habit), the boat will spin out quickly and stop.
- If you put the draw too far back and pull too hard on it toward the stern, you will overpower the spin-momentum and turn the boat to the left.

Drill 2: Do the same thing, but use a slightly (10 to 20 degrees) closed-face stern draw. You'll notice that you glide farther and the boat doesn't slow down as fast.

Why? Because the paddle is sailing you forward as well as keeping you from sliding. But then how does the paddle act as a sail? When you are turning, your kayak is trying to slide to the outside of the turn. Your draw stroke has blade pressure on it, which keeps you from sliding. When you have your paddle closed-face, the blade pressure propels your boat forward, like a sail. If you were to have an open-face blade, the sail would slow you down instead of speeding you up.

After a left stroke, my boat is rotating to the right. Prepare for a draw on the right immediately.

Put closed-face stern draw in the water and begin pulling toward the boat with enough pressure to keep the boat from sliding.

Boat should be turning right and gliding nicely without losing much speed.

Still gliding around the turn, looking to the inside of the turn.

Begin to turn the closed-face draw into a normal-face as the blade nears the side of the kayak.

You are now pointed in the direction you want to go and are almost ready to "feather forward" with your blade.

Blade feathering forward to prepare for a forward stroke to carry on propelling yourself forward and into your next move.

Paddle blade has been feathered to your toes, and you can now take a hard forward stroke to get where you are going.

Drill 3: I call this drill the Before and After Test. You'll need a partner for it. The drill is to paddle up to your partner, around the stern of their boat, and then back to where you came from. The goal is to use the minimum number of strokes, from the time your body passes their body going toward them to the time your body passes theirs coming back away from them. When I do this test with my students (which I do almost every time I teach a clinic), they range from 1 to 10 strokes, with about 5 being the average. Those who do it in 1 stroke have taken my strokes and concepts classes before and are getting quite proficient. Not only can you do it in a single stroke, but you can come out of the turn with more speed with 1 proper stroke than a person who does 5 hard strokes. This is a great example of the power of efficient paddling. The reason why 1 stroke can be faster and go as far as 5 strokes is that the person doing 5 strokes is letting their boat slide around the corner, and the person doing it in one stroke is carving the turn and carrying their speed around the turn using a proper draw stroke. If you can't easily do it in one stroke and come out of the turn with speed, you don't have a functional draw stroke yet, meaning you are still paddling with a limited repertoire of strokes.

THE STEERING WHEEL FOR YOUR KAYAK: THE POSITION OF THE DRAW STROKE

The exact position and pressure you put on the draw stroke (how hard you pull it toward the boat) determine how it affects your turning. If you want the boat to turn slower, move the draw stroke back toward the stern, but if you want the boat to turn faster, then move the draw stroke forward. Remember, however, that if the draw stroke gets in front of your butt, your stern will slide out and you'll lose your momentum.

The Fourth Rule of Turning

The fourth rule for turning is that you should always control each turn with the paddle on the inside of the turn, and use a draw stroke.

To recap, we now have four rules for every turn:
1. Look at your target.
2. Lead the turn with your body.
3. Control the turn with the paddle blade on the inside of the turn.
4. Use a draw stroke to control the turn.

Before you learn what it actually looks like to follow these four rules in your paddling, you will learn a few more strokes that use spin-momentum and draw strokes in them. We are getting into a new realm of paddle strokes now: compound strokes.

Compound Strokes

Combining a propulsion stroke with a draw stroke allows you to both propel yourself as well as control your turns effectively. The strokes in this section are the difference between needing 5 strokes for a move or just 1 stroke.

C-Stroke

C-stroke on whitewater.

The C-stroke is a combination of a closed-face bow draw and a forward stroke.

Remember the drill where you paddled around in a circle using only the inside strokes and spin-momentum to keep yourself turning toward your paddle? The C-stroke is used in the same type of situation, where you want to propel yourself forward but also control the radius of the turn using some amount of bow draw.

DRILL

1 big circle and 1 little circle in each direction
Attempt to make the big circle so big that it almost seems to be a straight line.

THE STROKE

Head: Look at your target, which is toward the inside of the turn, where you want your boat to go next.

Body: Lead the turn—lean toward the side of the boat you are doing the strokes on and turning toward.

Boat: Keep the boat flat so that you know you are using your stroke to keep the boat carving, and don't confuse yourself by thinking that keeping the boat on edge is what is making it carve and turn.

Paddle: Put the paddle into the water at your knees, about 2 feet from the boat and with a 45-degree closed face. Pull the closed-face draw straight into your knee, and then straighten the paddle out. Pull backward with a normal forward stroke. Make sure your top hand is over the bottom hand and that your paddle is completely vertical. Pull the paddle out at your butt, and repeat. When you put the closed face draw in the water and pull toward your knee you should feel like you're both propelling the boat forward (you are sculling the boat forward with this stroke) and also turning the boat in a tighter turn than if you had only used a forward stroke and didn't include the closed-face draw.

Closed-face bow draw starts the c-stroke.

Paddle moves toward toes to draw the bow and propel you forward.

Blade reaches boat at bow, and it is time to turn the closed-face draw into a forward stroke.

Blade is in forward stroke position and begins to pull you ahead.

Blade stays next to boat on forward stroke.

Completing forward stroke.

COMMON MISTAKES FOR THE C-STROKE

1. You didn't get spin-momentum going in the direction you want to pad-dle before you started. You have your paddle on the wrong side of the boat. If you are turning left, the left blade should be in the water doing the C-strokes.

2. You are not using a closed-face draw, but instead using an open-face or normal draw. Remember that you are trying to propel the boat forward during your active closed-face draw. For that reason, 45 degrees is the easiest angle to start at. If you use an open face, you will stop the boat dead in the water, and the stroke won't work.

3. You are sliding out before you get started because you can't get the stroke in the water before your boat slides and stops. Practice the position of the stroke without moving your kayak so that you can automatically get the stroke in the water right away on your next try.

4. You are not using a vertical paddle and are overpowering the spin-momentum during your forward stroke. If you are not going in a circle indefinitely and keeping the boat moving nicely in the direction of your paddle, you are overpowering your spin-momentum.

C-STROKE REVIEW

Level 1 Drill: Get the boat turning, and then use the C-stroke on the inside of the turn to complete a big circle first. To do a big circle, you need to use less draw and more forward stroke. Then, tighten up the radius of the turn by doing a harder, bigger closed-face draw and not pulling as long or hard on the forward stroke. Of course, after you get comfortable with it, you can do a circle with any radius you want.

See water trail of blade "actively moving toward boat."

Stroke complete at hip.

C-stroke draw.

C-stroke pull.

C-stroke finish.

C-stroke catch.

Level 2 Drill: Practice going through a series of turns in both directions. Imagine a maze or paddling through a group of kayakers. Use only the C-stroke to propel yourself forward and control the turns and a forward sweep to get the boat turning the other way when you want. Notice that you can really move around nicely using only the inside blade.

Level 3 Drill: Cross an eddy-line and C-stroke in a circle through the current and back into the eddy, up the eddy, and then back out again. You should be doing circles that have you crossing out into the current and back into the same eddy. Don't use any strokes except your C-stroke on the inside of the turn.

S-Turn Stroke

The S-turn stroke is a combination of a forward sweep, a closed-face stern draw, a "feather" forward of the paddle, and then a forward sweep to turn the boat the other way. Then you repeat: sweep, draw, feather forward, sweep, draw, feather forward. This stroke is the kayaking equivalent to carving a turn down a ski hill. Use this stroke to go from turning in one direction and carving that turn to turning in the other direction and carving that turn, too.

Carving across an eddy above the waterfalls at Rock Island on an S-turn stroke.

DRILL

S-turn back and forth 10 times

THE STROKE

There are several new skills you'll learn here that you should practice before you attempt to actually do this stroke.

THE "FEATHER"

Feathering is a kayaker's term for slicing your paddle through the water (instead of taking it out of the water) to reset it to a new position. The reason why you should feather the paddle in the S-turn stroke is that you can control the boat much better if your paddle is in the water during this turning stroke.

1. **Feather Drill:** Put your paddle in at the normal-face, stern draw position, and then feather it to your toes and back again. Try this quickly over and over again until you stop banging your paddle against the side of the boat and can keep it under control.
2. **Feather to Sweep Drill:** Now try the same thing, but instead of feathering the paddle back to your draw, convert the paddle to a sweep stroke. Feather forward, then sweep the bow. Try this a few times until you can do it without hesitation.

THE QUICK DRAW

In order to do a good S-turn stroke, you need to be able to go from a forward sweep on the left side to a draw on the right side with little hesitation. This technique is called the "quick draw." If you can't make the switch quickly or if you place the draw in the wrong position, you will not have a successful S-turn stroke. The draw must be a closed-face stern draw.

1. **Quick Draw Drill:** Do a forward sweep on your left, and then, as fast as you can, switch to a closed-face stern draw on the right. Double-check that your draw is going behind your butt (because it most likely isn't), and double-check that it is closed-face, not open-face, (again, because it most likely isn't). Repeat on the other side, and keep going until you can make the switch without any pause and without misplacing the paddle.

OK, you are almost ready to try your first S-turn strokes! If you're doing it correctly, your boat should move back and forth in an S-shape while keeping the forward momentum going. The longer the boat, the less the boat will turn on each stroke and the stronger your sweep stroke needs to be. A shorter boat, like a playboat, doesn't need a very strong forward sweep to change the spin-momentum from one direction to the other. You can use more of a forward stroke to overpower the spin-momentum. If you keep the total amount of turning to about 45 degrees each way, it will be easier to keep the forward speed going. Most people are too slow on the draw and end up turning 90 degrees each way and having no speed.

Head: Look at your target, which will change from one side to the other on each turn. Look over your right side when you have your left sweep stroke in position and keep looking right during your right draw. When you feather forward to sweep the boat back to the left, switch your head to look over the left side. (Remember, always look at your target.)

Body: Your body leads every turn. As with the head, you will need to switch your body from facing over one side of the boat to the other on each stroke. When you are feathering forward for your sweep, change your body position to lead the upcoming turn.

Boat: Keep the boat flat on this drill as well.

Paddle: Sweep to a quick closed-face stern draw, then glide on the draw for 3 seconds, then feather forward for a sweep the other way. Quick draw, glide for 3 seconds, then feather again, and continue.

Begin sweep on right.

Looking left.

Quick draw to a closed-face bow draw on left.

Glide on draw until you have turned 45 degrees to the left.

Begin feathering forward along boat.

Begin turning head and body to the right to prepare for a turn to the right.

With head and body leading, turn the boat the the right.

Boat is now rotating right. Begin quick draw on the right.

Right draw enters the water keeping the boat carving and turning right.

Applying pressure on the blade toward the boat helps propel the boat forward.

Begin feathering the blade forward, and repeat process.

COMMON MISTAKES FOR THE QUICK DRAW

1. You're too slow on the draw, so the boat spins out and slides to a stop.
2. Your draw stroke goes in too far forward (anywhere in front of your butt), so the boat slides out and stops.
3. Your draw stroke isn't closed face, so it stops the boat.
4. Your feathering is not smooth and causes drag that slows and stops the boat and gets it out of control.
5. You aren't gliding on the draw and carving the turn.

S-TURN STROKE REVIEW

Level 1 Drill: Make 10 turns in each direction. Focus on keeping the boat moving, feeling the glide on the draw, a smooth feather, and a quick draw.

Level 2 Drill: Make 10 turns in each direction, but throw in a few C-strokes in between each S-turn stroke to get some more speed and distance while turning in one direction before turning back the other way. Basically, take charge of making the boat go where you want it to go using only S-turns and C-strokes.

Level 3 Drill: Practice your S-turn strokes in whitewater, crossing mid-current eddies and gliding on the draw across them, sweeping and heading downriver. Focus more on the draw on either side and less on the sweeps since you have the speed of the river.

Reverse Compound Stroke

This is your first backward stroke that also uses spin-momentum. It is a wonderful stroke for improving paddle dexterity, spin-momentum control, feathering, and your awareness when moving backward. If you want to paddle backward efficiently, this stroke allows you to carry your speed around turns while moving backward. It is also the easiest way to cross an eddy-line backward. The reverse compound stroke makes paddling backward much easier, and you will be much more comfortable and effective after you master it.

DRILL

1 big circle and 1 little circle in each direction

THE STROKE

The reverse compound stroke is a combination of an open-face reverse stroke with the power face toward you, flipping the paddle over at the hip for a normal reverse stroke, and then feathering back to the open-face reverse stroke again. The stroke also has a gliding component after the feather where you glide backward on an open-face bow draw (but because you are going backward, it is really like doing a closed-face stern draw).

Reach behind you with the power face down.

After a short power face down pull, flip the blade over for a normal reverse stroke.

Keep paddle blade next to boat on reverse stroke.

Convert forward stroke into open-face bow draw and begin feathering to the starting position again.

Feathering to the stern for next stroke.

You are going to learn the mechanics of the stroke first before you learn how to include spin-momentum.

Head: The head looks back where you are going. Turn your head and body as far to the back as you can so you can see clearly.

Body: You will be using torso rotation in the beginning when alternating left and right reverse compound strokes, but you will be leading with your body during the spin-momentum drill.

Boat: Keep the boat flat.

Paddle: When learning the mechanics, keep the power face toward you. Spoon down, reaching as far back to the stern as you can next to the boat. Do a short pull from your stern to almost your hip. Flip the blade over 180 degrees to get into a normal backward stroke position. Push yourself backward with a reverse stroke until your blade is at your toes. Now take the paddle out, and try on the other side.

Once you can do that successfully, you can add feathering and spin-momentum to complete this stroke the proper way (being able to paddle backward and control spin-momentum with one blade). Start off the same: pull with a short power face–down reverse stroke, flip the blade over, and then push yourself backward with a normal reverse stroke. Now, feather your blade back to the original position and do it again.

Reverse compound stroke reach.

Reverse compound stroke pull.

Reverse compound flip.

Reverse compound finish push.

Reverse compound feather draw.

Reverse compound feather.

Reverse compound flip again.

Reverse compound finish feather.

REVERSE COMPOUND STROKE REVIEW

Level 1 Drill: Do 10 strokes on each side, going in a straight line backward, alternating between left and right blade. Don't feather back.

Level 2 Drill: Do a big circle and a little circle backward, paddling on only one side. Paddle backward, get your speed going, and then get the boat spinning toward the direction you want to turn. Now reach back power face–down, pull, flip, push, feather back into position, and continue. You should be able to keep the speed up and keep carving the boat.

Level 3 Drill: Add an open-face bow draw to the end of you reverse stroke before you feather back. Glide on the draw for 3 seconds, and then feather back and repeat with another stroke. Practice controlling your glide with the open-face bow draw.

Gliding on an open-face bow draw is a great way to control your boat when going backward.

Offside C-Stroke

Here is a stroke that seems like a "trick stroke" to most people when I first introduce them to it. While the offside C-stroke isn't necessary to be able to kayak down a river, the paddlers who learn it certainly have a major advantage over the paddlers who don't. First off, it is a wonderful paddle dexterity exercise: It makes you very good at controlling your blade angles and feathering. It is also a great spin-momentum exercise, which you'll appreciate as you begin to use spin-momentum to your advantage. Finally, if you were to break a paddle on the river, this stroke allows you to paddle without switching hands, and to get down the river with one blade. And yes, it is also a cool stroke to show your friends.

DRILL

1 big circle, 1 little circle in each direction

THE STROKE

The offside C-stroke is the first stroke where you paddle with the blade on the wrong side of the boat. You use your right blade on the left side of the boat. This stroke also includes feathering back into position instead of taking the paddle out of the water.

Head: Your head leads the turn—so look where you are paddling the kayak next.

Boat: Keep your boat flat.

Body: Keep your weight over the boat and your body leading the turn.

Paddle: Because this is a spin-momentum drill, get the boat moving forward with speed. Start it spinning to the right. Now, place your left paddle on the right side of the boat, and pull yourself forward with an offside forward stroke. Quickly turn the paddle so the power face is toward the boat, and feather forward and away from the kayak. Now pull the paddle toward the boat and convert the paddle back into a forward stroke, and then repeat. Keep your top hand over the bottom hand for maximum power and effectiveness.

Boat is moving forward and spinning left as I put my right blade in on the left side of the boat to begin the C-stroke.

Vertical paddle pulling the boat forward.

At the hip, turn your paddle blade into feathering position and begin feathering back to bow.

COMMON MISTAKES FOR THE OFFSIDE C-STROKE

1. You put the paddle on the outside of the turn instead of the inside. You will know you did this because your boat will stop dead and just spin in a circle without going anywhere.

2. You struggle with feathering forward and losing your speed due to a poor feather angle. To fix this, you need to practice the feather back and forth to get the feeling right so that you are not banging the boat.

3. You are not punching forward with the top hand far enough to create a vertical paddle. If your top hand is too far back and your bottom hand is up by your toes, the stroke will be very weak, and you won't go far or fast. Punch the top hand over the bottom hand for a strong stroke.

4. You are not getting enough speed to start or you're waiting too long to begin pulling yourself forward. Your boat will spin out and stop if you do that.

5. You are not leading with your body. Leading with your body will help you comfortably use the paddle on the offside and help keep the turn going.

Paddle blade feathering back to starting position vertically.

Forward stroke next to boat pulling you forward again.

OFFSIDE C-STROKE REVIEW

Level 1: Make 1 big circle and 1 little circle in both directions. Focus on forward speed during the big circles and really focus on a strong bow draw during the little circles.

Level 2: Paddle the boat around where you want, using only offside C-strokes, and switching sides when you are ready to turn the other direction. Use an offside sweep stroke to change the spin-momentum. Really focus on the speed of the kayak on the bigger turns, and practice going from a tight turn back to a big turn where you go fast again, all without losing spin-momentum.

Level 3: Cross an eddy-line using the offside C-stroke, and then keep the boat turning, heading downstream. Then, head back into the eddy again, crossing the eddy-line for an eddy out—all without taking the paddle out of the water. Paddle up the eddy again and back out of the top of the eddy, still staying on the inside of the turn and using only the offside C-stroke.

Sideslip Stroke

This is the first open-face draw stroke you'll be able to use while going forward. The sideslip stroke allows you to draw the boat sideways while still moving forward (and without having to make a turn) and then keep going in the direction you were headed. Basically, it is a way to side-step obstacles or to slip sideways out of an eddy, onto a wave, or wherever you like.

DRILL

2 side-slips each direction

THE STROKE

This is a nearly static stroke. Although you will have forward speed to start, you'll throw in an open-face stern draw and hold the paddle tight in that position. The paddle will try to track away from the edge of the kayak in the direction it is pointed. Instead of letting the paddle get farther from the kayak, hold it tight to pull the entire kayak sideways.

The sideslip stroke is, believe it or not, a spin-momentum exercise as well. While you are trying to pull the boat sideways and not "turn," the reality is that the boat must be spinning toward the paddle or it won't work.

Head: Look where you want to slip the boat to: your target.

Boat: Keep the boat flat to slide the easiest.

Body: Rotate your body to the side of the boat you are slipping (turning) to.

Paddle: This is a static stroke unless you need to move the paddle to keep the boat straight. You will paddle forward to get as much speed as possible and get the boat rotating slightly in the direction you want to slip toward. Throw your open-face stern draw in the water to keep the boat from turning, but don't overpower the spin-momentum. Hold the paddle tight, and drag your boat sideways. If your boat spins toward the side your paddle is on, your paddle was too far forward. If your boat spins away from the side your paddle is on, you were too far back, or you pulled too hard on the draw.

Open-face draw at hip or stern when moving forward pulls boat sideways.

Blade angle is only slightly open to prevent stopping the boat.

See rocks moving off to the side as boat is slipping to the right.

SIDESLIP STROKE REVIEW

Level 1: Make 2 sideslips in each direction in flatwater.

Level 2: Practice sideslipping around a friend—start on their left, paddle hard toward them, and then slip past their boat to the right side. Slip back to the left side again after you pass them.

Level 3: Practice slipping around rocks in the river. Paddling downstream on the right side of a rock, slip to the left side of it without turning the boat. Also practice slipping into position into slots without turning the boat.

Reverse Sweep Torso Drill

DRILL

30 alternating reverse sweeps:
(10 slow, 10 medium, 10 fast)

This drill is amazing for strengthening your torso, stretching out your ribs, pecs, biceps, and neck, and for helping you learn to separate your torso from your hips. It's also an effective initiation stroke for playboating.

PADDLE POSITION AND MOVEMENT

While this drill is simply a series of alternating reverse sweeps, for maximum effect, the timing is key. Do a full reverse sweep on one side, pause until your boat has rotated at least 90 degrees, and then put in a full reverse sweep on the other side. In order for this drill to be effective, your back arm must be totally straight, and you must reach as far to the stern as you can without leaning back. Push the paddle straight away from the stern to maximize the sweeping effect.

BODY POSITION AND MOVEMENT

Keep your body in a neutral or forward position; don't lean back. When you put the paddle in the water to start your reverse sweep, rotate your head and body as far as possible so that you can see your stern and so that your torso is fully wound up. You will feel your stomach, ribs, neck, biceps (if you are keeping your back arm straight), and pectoral muscles stretching when you start your reverse sweep. Start slowly, and gradually build up the amount of effort you put into each stroke so that you don't pull a muscle. Accentuate your body rotation during each stroke so that you get maximum warm-up and stretching effect. This is a critical stretch before playboating because it warms and stretches the muscles that are at the highest risk of injury.

Reach back with extended rear arm, full torso rotation, and head turned as far as it can go on each stroke.

BOAT POSITION AND MOVEMENT

Lean your boat to the inside of the turn slightly so that you initiate the bow underwater on each sweep. The tendency for many kayakers is to rock back and forth on each stroke. This shows either that you aren't paying attention or that you can't move your body without having the boat move with it. This drill will help you separate your body and boat motions. This separation is critical for slalom, extreme boating, and playboating because you often need to rotate, look, lean, or duck, but your boat must stay on course and flat. You also need to control where your boat is heading. You should be able to go in a straight line while your boat is zigzagging.

Squirt Stroke

THE STROKE

The squirt stroke is really just a reverse sweep, but it includes some edge control and weight control to make the stern of the boat go underwater and to make the boat rotate around and pivot underwater.

DRILL

Paddle forward, sweep your boat to 90 degrees, and then do a strong reverse sweep while dropping the outside edge of your kayak and lifting up on your knees. If your stern goes underwater and the bow lifts and rotates around 270 degrees, you did it! You can draw the bow around the last 90 degrees to complete the 360-degree turn.

Why learn the squirt stroke? Because it's fun! Also squirting is an edge control exercise that will help you use edges to your advantage instead of having them cause you issues. Learning the squirt stroke will also ensure that you can squirt your boat vertical on eddy-lines!

Head: Lead the turn—look in the direction you intend to turn the boat.

Boat: You will want to drop about 30 degrees of edge to get the boat to go underwater. The shorter the boat, the more edge you need to drop: 20 degrees for a slalom boat, 45 degrees for a new playboat.

Body: Your body leads the turn. Rotate as far as you physically can in the direction you are going to squirt in.

Paddle: You have three strokes to do to complete a 360-degree stern squirt.

1. First, get some speed forwards and then *forward sweep* the boat to 90 degrees to the direction you are traveling.
2. *Reverse sweep* hard, starting at or behind the stern of your kayak.
3. *Draw* the boat around for the final 90 degrees with an open-face bow draw.

One hundred percent full extension on arm and torso is best position for squirt stroke catch.

Boat edge down at 45 degrees and full power on reverse sweep will allow stern to be pushed under the water.

Completed stern squirt means blade power is no longer needed as the boat is completely submerged and rotating on its own.

SQUIRT STROKE REVIEW

Level 1 Drill: Paddle forward and stern squirt, and then draw it around to 360 degrees. Repeat three times each way.

Level 2 Drill: Paddle forward and stern squirt to vertical in flatwater. Try to bring it down without having to roll (draw the bow around, and turn it into a high brace).

Level 3 Drill: Try stern squirting on an eddy-line: paddle up to the eddy-line at 90 degrees to the eddy-line. Eliminate the forward sweep, but still back sweep and drop your edge at the moment your butt crosses the eddy-line. Try to reach around for a draw to keep you upright, and turn that into a high brace.

Initiation Stroke for Playboating

While the initiation stroke is designed to get you cartwheeling your playboat, it is also one of the most amazing drills for edge control, weight over the boat, and stroke timing that has ever been invented.

To do the initiation stroke drill, put your boat on edge, at a 45-degree angle, and rock it back and forth so that the bow and stern bob up and down in the water. The purpose of the drill is to learn how to push your bow underwater to get a cartwheel going and also how to pull the stern underwater to get a cartwheel going. If you can't get the ends of your boat underwater on demand, you won't be able to cartwheel. This drill teaches you to balance in the cartwheel position and to have good, strong initiation strokes. Every boat bobs at a different rate, so you must understand your boat's natural rate and not fight its natural movement.

PADDLE POSITION AND MOVEMENT

With your paddle in the forward sweep position, sweep your bow into the air. (Since your boat is on edge, the bow will go up instead of off to the side.) Immediately push your top hand in front of you so that you are in a reverse sweep position, and then push the bow back down with a reverse sweep. Repeat over and over: push-pull, push-pull with your paddle. The key is to be quick. Beginners tend to push and pull with off timing, because the boat wants to bob up and down at a rate faster than they are stroking. Think of it this way: You sweep your stern under, and the air in the stern makes it pop back out of the water. Your goal is to assist that process by doing a back sweep that helps lift the stern out and push the bow in. When the bow goes in, you want to help it get back up to the surface and help the stern get back under. In general, the pace is about two bobs per second. If you are going slower than that, your boat will not respond, as you will be fighting the floatation of the boat instead of being in resonance with it.

Blade pulls down, lifting bow up at 45 degrees in front, out to the side, and blade angle is power face down 45 degrees pointed back.

Switch blade to power face up and push bow down with back stroke.

Quick changes from forward to reverse sweep strokes should cause paddle blade to scull on the surface of the water.

Blade action acts like a brace as well as causing boat to rock on edge, preparing you to learn cartwheels.

CHAPTER 7

Applying the Strokes and Concepts to Whitewater

You now know everything you need to know about performing kayaking strokes in flatwater. This is exciting because it means you know all of the strokes for whitewater as well. You will now learn how to apply the strokes to whitewater. The flatwater drills are the only way to learn the strokes quickly and to improve them each time you paddle. Applying the strokes to whitewater comes automatically in many cases, but there are still some drills that will help you quite a bit. To be proficient in whitewater, you need control, efficiency, consistency, simplicity, and speed. Just as in flatwater, where learning to use the draw properly can reduce the number of strokes you need, learning proper whitewater techniques can reduce the number of strokes you need—allowing you to go faster and have more control.

Four Whitewater Concepts

Whitewater has energy that you can harness with your boat and paddle. The faster the water, the more energy. In kayaking there are two sources of energy to direct and propel your boat: your own energy and the river's energy. The best kayakers use a combination of both.

Current itself isn't enough energy to propel your boat. For instance, if you are floating down a fast-moving flat river, then relative to the water, you are stationary. However, every time you cross a current differential, you do have potential energy that you can harness with the right speed, angle, arc, spin-momentum, and paddle strokes. The places where there are current differentials are eddy-lines, holes, or waves.

The four concepts I will focus on are:

1. **Speed:** The velocity of your kayak, either forward or backward relative to the water. For example, having speed out of an eddy means you paddled hard while in the eddy and are crossing the eddy-line with speed.
2. **Angle:** The angle of your boat relative to an eddy-line, the current in a wave, the backwash of a hole, or the current in a hole.
3. **Spin-Momentum:** The direction in which your kayak is spinning when it is moving forward or backward.
4. **Arc:** The path your body and boat take, from a bird's-eye view. All moves in whitewater are most efficiently done in an arc, never in a straight line.

Eddy Turns

Let's begin applying the strokes and concepts to whitewater with eddy turns. You can use eddy turns to go in or out of an eddy.

THE STROKES

1. Use forward strokes up to and while pulling yourself across the eddy-line, with a final forward stroke on the downstream side that starts before your butt hits the eddy-line and finishes after your butt is across the eddy-line.
2. Convert the forward stroke into a closed-face stern draw.

DRILL

Peel out of an eddy and carve a turn until you are facing downstream. After establishing yourself, turn your boat back toward the eddy. Eddy out using the same technique you used to peel out, and then glide on the stern draw to get as deep into the eddy as you can. Practice entering the eddy at different angles. The goal of an eddy turn is to have a smooth, wide arc on the exit (upstream to crosscurrent to downstream momentum) and on the reentry (downstream to crosscurrent to upstream momentum). Accelerate on your draw using the river's energy.

Get your speed and angle set.

Take forward stroke across eddy-line.

Ride stern draw into position.

Locking in.

Feather forward and prepare final locking stroke.

Final locking stroke.

Choose your speed and angle to approach eddy-line.

Reach across eddy-line for peel out.

Pull your forward stroke into a closed-face stern draw on peel out.

Ride the closed-face stern draw to your target.

The boat should travel with speed to your target with only the draw stroke.

The following are some common misconceptions about eddy turns.

Misconception: You should do a sweep to turn the boat into the eddy.

Explanation: It is risky to wait until you are right at the eddy to turn your boat into the eddy. You would have to turn the boat at exactly the right time and get the proper angle, all while trying to cross the eddy-line, which is difficult.

If you set your angle upstream of the eddy, you can just float until you are in the right position and then take two or three strokes to get to the eddy-line. You don't have time to turn; you can do it well in advance and then focus on hitting the eddy-line at the precise spot you have chosen.

Misconception: You should bow draw into the eddy.

Explanation: Bow draws (with an open face—as they are typically done when people use them to eddy out) slow your boat down and cause the stern to slide out. They counteract your primary goal of converting your downstream and crosscurrent momentum into upstream momentum to "lock" into the eddy. Instead, pick the angle and speed across the eddy-line that allows you to draw at the hip and lock into the eddy. If you don't keep your draw at the hip when you cross the eddy, you will slide downstream. You have both downstream and crosscurrent momentum when entering an eddy, and you need to convert that momentum into upstream momentum. That requires a proper draw to convert your speed around the turn and back upstream.

There are many situations that make for less-than-ideal eddy turns. Be sure to practice using techniques that are as close to ideal as possible. When approaching a small, narrow eddy with no room to glide deep into it, come in pointed straight to shore, with lots of crosscurrent speed but little downstream speed. Pull yourself across the eddy-line into the normal draw position, pull hard toward the boat on the draw for an instant to lock in, and then immediately feather the blade to your knees and do a C-stroke to lock in. Big water eddy-lines with big boils make the crossing of the eddy-line challenging and the timing of the draw harder. The key to timing it is to make sure you put the draw stroke in water that will apply pressure to the power face of the blade. For example, the back side of a boil will do it.

Ferrying

THE STROKES

1. Use a forward stroke to pull yourself across the eddy-line.
2. Convert that into a closed-face stern draw.

FERRYING DRILL 1

Practice ferrying out as far as possible with one stroke, using different boat and blade angles to learn the effect of each and to be able to intuitively pick the right speed, angle, arc, spin-momentum, and draw position to get where you want to go. The goal is to ferry under control and to use the current to accelerate your boat across the river to the destination of your choice with one stroke.

Ferrying is moving across the river using the river's energy to drive your kayak to the desired destination. It's a way to paddle from one side of the river to the other without losing much or any ground. There is no difference between an eddy turn and a ferry in terms of general theory and technique. A ferry requires the same speed, angle, and spin-momentum necessary for a good peel-out, so you should use the same strokes. The fundamental difference between an eddy turn and a ferry is the path of the arc: Rather than gradually converting upstream momentum into downstream momentum, as you would for an eddy turn, you convert the upstream momentum into crosscurrent momentum.

When you exit an eddy on fairly stable water with no huge boils, you should be able to ferry to any destination you want with a single draw stroke. This is true for most rivers that flow at less than 5,000 cubic feet per second and are less than 75 feet wide. Larger rivers will require that you start paddling again with forward strokes to get to the other side. Crossing on one stroke may seem impossible if you haven't tried it or seen anyone else do it, but it really works! You will eliminate 4 to 6 strokes from each peel-out or ferry, have much greater control, and have much more speed to your destination.

FERRYING DRILL 2

Get speed and angle set for ferry.

Reach across eddy-line.

Convert forward stroke to closed.

Boat should maintain upstream.

Spot target and prepare to catch.

Allow bow to drop into eddyout.

Switch to other blade to begin.

Eddyout begins.

Locking into eddy after ferry.

Get up speed in the eddy, using forward strokes, and approach the eddy-line at a 45-degree angle. Reach across the eddy-line, and pull your butt across it with a forward stroke. Convert the forward stroke into a closed-face stern draw. Apply pressure to the stroke by holding the stern draw close to the boat. The current will try to drag your paddle away from your boat. Hold the paddle in position so that the water will pull your paddle, boat, and body across the river and accelerate you, just like wind in a sail. The size of your arc is determined by the position of your paddle. If it is far back to the stern and you are holding a lot of pressure on it, you will not turn downstream at all but will ferry. If you have it close to the center of the boat (your butt), you will turn quickly downstream and won't be able to ride the draw as long. It's your job to keep the draw at your stern long enough to get as far as you want across the river and then to feather the paddle forward to let the bow turn downstream. Remember that you want a smooth, steady arc. If you turn quickly downstream after leaving the eddy, you can forget gliding, efficiency, and speed. If you make a quick 180-degree turn after the ferry, you won't be using the current at all. Take a wide arc out of the eddy by holding the stern draw until you are far enough out into the current for your next destination. Your draw can move forward or backward to keep the boat on the path you want. The instant you take the draw out of the water, you are no longer in control or using the river's energy, so don't take it out until you have completely turned downstream or you want to turn the other way.

When ferrying onto waves, use the same technique, staying on the stern draw until you have established yourself on the wave.

FERRYING INTO AN EDDY

Often you'll have to ferry into an eddy, such as when you are playboating or catching an eddy that you saw too late. When ferrying into an eddy, the eddy-line will tend to reject your boat and prevent you from getting into the eddy. You need to get your entire boat past the eddy-line. The forward stroke across the eddy-line is the same for a normal eddy turn. Keep the bow pointed toward the shore by pulling (and sweeping) on the upstream side only, until you are completely in the eddy. Try to avoid being turned parallel to the eddy-line.

Whitewater S-Turns

You can do an S-turn in whitewater across eddies that are in the middle of the river so that there is current on both sides of the eddy. Simply go in one side of the eddy and come out the other. The S-turn is the fastest, most efficient way to get from one side of the river to another. Any time you are running a rapid and there are eddies in the middle of the river, you have an opportunity to use those eddies to get where you want to go without many strokes. The ideal S-turn starts the same as a regular eddy turn. You begin with a downstream angle and pull yourself across the eddy-line with a forward stroke that turns into a stern draw. Keep the draw in the water and your boat pointed straight across the eddy toward the far shore until you reach the other side of the eddy. Convert your draw into a forward stroke and pull. Then, reach across the eddy-line with your other blade, and use the standard peel-out technique, consisting of a forward stroke that turns into a stern draw in the current as you head back downstream. You can glide across most eddies in one stroke. The S-turn in whitewater is very much like the S-turn stroke drill in flatwater. It is actually much easier to keep the boat moving because of the energy you pick up when you cross the eddy-line.

WHITEWATER S-TURN REVIEW

Level 1 Drill: Enter the eddy as you would for a normal eddy turn. Keep your bow pointed at the far shore until you hit the next eddy-line. When you cross the eddy-line on the way out, switch to a forward stroke that turns into a stern draw, as you would for a normal peel-out.

Level 2 Drill: Put your boat slightly on the inside edge of the eddy on the way in, and then again on the way out. Extreme leans are not necessary or beneficial. Pick an arc that gives you the peel-out angle you want when you get to the other side of the eddy. For example, if you wanted to cross the eddy and then ferry to the other side of the river, you would allow the bow to turn up more in the eddy so that you would exit the eddy with a good ferry angle. Practice gliding across the eddy with a closed-face stern draw. You can keep up your speed that way.

Level 3 Drill: Practice using all kinds of holes ot S-turn, such as the back-wash of pour-overs or flat holes. The trick is to lean into the turn (upstream) on the entry. You need to get your boat on top of the backwash so that you don't catch your upstream edge. If you lean downstream when you hit the hole, you'll stop dead, catch your downstream edge, and have to brace. Paddle with speed to the corner of the hole, and jump on top from a 45-degree angle. As soon as your boat hits the foam pile, you should begin leaning upstream and pull yourself on top of the hole, using a forward stroke that feathers into a draw on the upstream side of your boat.

Surfing Holes

For many beginner, intermediate, and even expert kayakers, the scariest parts of a river run are holes. We fear the unknown: Will that hole stop me? If I get surfed, will I be able to get out? Can I roll in a hole? Most kayakers don't have enough experience with holes to know what to expect, so they try to avoid holes. But if avoiding holes becomes a habit, you'll have a problem. There are only so many features in a river that you can use: the current, waves, rocks, eddies, and holes. If you spend your kayaking career avoiding holes, you are very limited in what rivers and creeks you can run, and you won't be prepared when you do surf a hole.

Planing hull (flat-bottom) boats are wider and generally more stable in holes than are displacement hull (curved-bottom) boats. This is accentuated when they are planing (sitting on top of the green water instead of inside it) due to the water rushing under them when you are sitting sideways in a hole. They also have less resistance to the oncoming water when sideways, so they don't get pushed into the foam pile as far. Displacement hulled boats get pushed into the foam. The foam lifts them up, takes them back upstream, and then drops them in the green water—and then the cycle repeats. It is a much bouncier ride and much harder to control.

To overcome your fear of holes and make the most of them, you first need to understand the characteristics of a hole before you enter it. Once you've entered a hole, you need to know how to stay upright, how to roll, and how to get out.

UNDERSTANDING THE HOLE BEFORE YOU ENTER IT

There are three kinds of holes. I'll call them **wave holes**, **simple holes**, and **pour-over holes**.

Entering hole with a closed-face brace.

Bracing and moving with a closed-face brace.

Keeping weight over boat.

Putting more pressure on paddle to move forward faster.

In the meat.

Pulling out with a closed-face brace and momentum.

Almost out.

Weight over boat and paddle away.

A **wave hole** occurs when the oncoming water goes down into a trough and, upon rising, falls back onto itself, creating a foam pile on top of the wave. This kind of hole is easiest to surf because the oncoming water approaches smoothly and at a low angle. Also, it is frequently more difficult to stay in a wave hole than it is to get out. This type of hole is the best bet for learning hole-surfing techniques.

A **simple hole** occurs where the oncoming water meets the foam pile at the trough of the hole, yet the oncoming water approaches at an angle of 60 degrees or less.

A **pour-over hole** occurs where the water drops almost vertically off a ledge or over a rock to form a hole that has significant backwash and very little water flowing downstream through it. It is more difficult to brace and maneuver in a pour-over because you have to lean so far downstream to avoid catching your upstream edge.

STAYING UPRIGHT

A hole tends to want to hold you sideways in it. It also wants to grab your upstream edge and flip you upstream. In order to stay upright and be balanced, you need to lean your boat downstream so the hull is sitting flat on the oncoming water. For example, if the water coming into the hole is dropping at an angle of 30 degrees, then you need to lean your boat 30 degrees downstream so that the water planes off of the hull. If you lean your body too much downstream, you'll have to brace hard to stay upright. Keep your weight over the boat.

BRACING

Bracing in a hole is easy. The water going under your boat offers plenty of support for your brace. Either a high or low brace will keep your boat upright.

For a high brace, keep the paddle's power face down, keep your elbows under the paddle, and keep the paddle perpendicular to the boat. For a low brace, keep the paddle's back face against the water, keep your elbows over the paddle, and again keep the paddle perpendicular to the boat. Which brace you use will depend on whether you want to move your boat forward or backward. To move forward, use a high brace. To move backward, use a low brace. The brace should be in front of your body, and the paddle shaft should be perpendicular to your boat. It doesn't require much force on the paddle to stay upright if you are keeping your weight over the boat and keeping the boat angle the same as the water coming down into the hole.

ROLLING IN A HOLE

Rolling is easier in a hole than anywhere else, including flatwater. In a hole, the water tries to roll you back up; you only need to help it. If you feel yourself being tipped in a hole, the first thing to do is relax. Don't fight it. There's nothing you can do once you begin flipping upstream in a hole. If you try to brace as you're going over, you'll likely hit bottom with your paddle and either break it or hurt your shoulder. By relaxing, you are keeping your paddle still and perpendicular to your boat, and keeping your head forward and face down. Most of the time, flipping upstream in a hole is very safe, even if the hole is shallow. This is because the oncoming water pushes you downstream into the foam pile, and your boat pops up a bit when your body enters the water, keeping you in deeper water and your body shallow. Holes are very forgiving that way, and we can be grateful for that!

Once you've flipped over, the oncoming water will pull your body downstream and then try to lift up on the downstream side. This is the side you should roll up on. If you relax and keep your paddle on your spray skirt and perpendicular to the boat, you only have to brace with the paddle and do a hip snap to roll up. No fancy setup technique is required. You'll know you are trying to roll up on the wrong side if you can't get your paddle to go where you want it. Make sure to practice your offside hip snaps and braces, because you have a 50 percent chance of being on your off side. Even if you can't roll on both sides in flatwater, you'll be able to roll on both sides in a hole.

After you've rolled up, resume the bracing position. If you forget to lean your boat downstream after hip-snapping up, you'll keep rolling over upstream. This unpleasant, but fun-to-watch action is known as window-shading.

GETTING OUT OF A HOLE

In general, there are three places to exit a hole: at the end of the hole on river right, on river left, or out through the foam pile in the middle of it. Though there are multiple ways to get out of a hole, the one constant is that you must eventually get out of that hole, or you'll have to swim. Swimming is an option we won't discuss here. To get out of a hole is to understand how to maneuver in a hole. Depending on the type of hole, you may be able to pull out forward, back out, ender out, or blast out of the hole. Whether you go forward or backward, when you reach the edge, your boat will begin to turn downstream, and the oncoming water will try to catch your upstream edge and flip you upstream. This will tip you over, but it will also help you get out of the hole. Remember that tipping over is OK and can even be a good thing.

Pulling Out

If you want to pull yourself forward out of a hole, start with a high brace. Cock your right wrist down about 45 degrees, which will give you 50 percent bracing and 50 percent forward stroke with your paddle. If you push your paddle in the water, the water rushing downstream will pull you forward and support your brace. If you need more power to get out the side of the hole, you can raise your left arm to get the paddle more vertical, giving you more of a forward stroke to pull forward. Be careful, however, not to raise your hand too high above your shoulder, as you risk shoulder injury. You need enough momentum to get out of the hole, and the deeper the hole, the more momentum and power you'll need to get out of it. If you try to pull forward to get out, but you stall and can't pull yourself all the way out, don't worry. You just need to relax, let the hole bring you back into the trough, and start again, getting more momentum from the beginning to break out. If this doesn't work, then try backing out.

Backing Out

Backing out is similar to pulling out, except that you push backward with a low brace. Starting in the low brace position, cock your right wrist back 45 degrees, which will give you 50 percent bracing and 50 percent backstroke. Push the paddle into the water, and the oncoming water will give you support for bracing and allow you to push yourself backward. Try to create as much momentum as you can from the start to break out of the hole. You can alternate backing up and then pulling forward to get as much speed as possible.

Endering Out

It is also possible to have the downstream-flowing water push you out through the hole by launching you over the foam pile. This can be easy or difficult, depending on the hole. In order to ender out of a hole, you must be able to move to the side of the hole by high or low bracing and pulling yourself out to the side. Often, holes let you to the side easily but don't let you out the very end, because there's a hill to climb that slows your momentum. In this case, your boat will start to exit the hole and turn downstream, but you will get pulled back in, and your bow or stern will catch the oncoming water and be pushed underwater, catapulting your boat downstream. Most often, the ender is not vertical but is more of an upstream flip that gets your boat about 45 degrees into the air. Here, you'll usually vault over the foam pile and out of the hole.

Blasting Out

Blasting out of a hole is just surfing the hole, with the foam pile pushing on your back and the hull planing off the oncoming water. Think of blasting as front or back surfing the hole. The new shorter boats do this very easily with simple holes and wave holes, but it takes more skill to blast pour-overs. From this position, the oncoming water typically tries to surf you to one side or another with lots of speed. This allows you to use the energy in the foam pile and oncoming water, thus front-surfing right out of a hole without having to climb out. The technique is to do a powerful front sweep while you are side-surfing to force your stern under the foam pile. Lean back and continue your sweep into a stern draw to help get the stern under and the bow on top of the approaching water. Keep the stern draw in the water, and surf out the side. You need to practice blasting to learn to control it well.

Going Out the Bottom

To go out the bottom of a hole, you can let yourself flip upstream and hope you wash out. This works only for holes that have a non-retentive foam pile. The size of the hole isn't the determining factor, only the amount of water that goes through it versus the amount of water coming back upstream. If you don't wash out, you'll have to put your downstream paddle blade in the water and use a hip snap to roll back up.

HOLES REVIEW

STAYING UPRIGHT IN A HOLE
- Keep your weight centered over the boat.
- Keep your hull flat on the oncoming water. Lean your boat downstream to keep the upstream edge from catching.
- Keep your paddle in the water in either a high or low brace position.

MANEUVERING IN A HOLE
- Use a high brace with a closed face to pull yourself forward. Pull against the water, going under the foam pile.
- Use a low brace, and cock your wrist up and back so you can push yourself backward in the hole.

ROLLING IN A HOLE
- Relax and let yourself go when you feel yourself catching an edge and going over.
- Keep your paddle on your spray skirt and perpendicular to the boat. This sets you up for the roll.
- Keep your body forward with your head down when flipping over. Brace yourself back up on the downstream side with a high brace and a controlled hip snap.

Surfing Waves

This is not primarily a playboating book, so the goal in this section is to teach you how to control yourself on waves so you can use them in your river running. You need to practice ferrying and be comfortable with turning a forward stroke into a stern draw before you practice wave techniques. No matter what level you currently paddle at, you should use the peel-out technique to cross the eddy-line onto a wave.

There are three elements to surfing a wave: getting there, being there, and going somewhere else. The best way to get on a wave is from an eddy that allows you to peel out onto the wave from directly beside it. Ideally, your technique will put you on the wave and in control the first time, every time. To do this, you want to eliminate as many variables as possible before you cross the eddy-line, leaving only the minimum amount of maneuvering for when you're on the actual wave.

VARIABLES YOU MUST CONTROL
How far up or down the wave your boat is when you catch it.
- Your butt should be just in front of the peak of the wave as you enter the wave from the side. If it is way in front of the peak, in the trough, you'll have difficulty keeping your bow up and controlling the bow once you are on it. If you're behind the peak, you'll miss the wave entirely.
- You can eliminate this variable by peeling out of the eddy when your butt is just in front of the peak. You can always maintain control in the flatwater of an eddy. So before you start, pick the path out of the eddy that puts you where you need to be.

Whether your boat's momentum is going upstream or downstream.
- Ideally, you want to get on the wave from the side with no up- or downstream momentum. This way, you can get on the wave just in front of the peak and stay there.
- You control your speed while entering the wave by exiting the eddy in the right spot with the right speed. You wouldn't sprint across the eddy-line onto a wave that is easy to get to from the side, because you'd ride right down the face of the wave into the trough instantly. You need to cross the eddy-line with the right speed. It would be similar to jumping onto a moving treadmill. If you simply sprang up onto it, you'd be dragged right into the bars at the end. You would have to jump on it from the side while running the same speed as the treadmill was going.
- Once you have the necessary forward speed, you can reach across the eddy-line and pull yourself sideways onto the face of the wave.

What angle you have to the wave.
- You'll control your exit angle out of the eddy with your stern draw. If you're at an angle at which you could ferry across the river, then you're also at an angle that will work for surfing.

Which way your spin-momentum is going.

- When you get onto a wave, you'll surf right across to the other side and off it unless you turn back. With the stern draw in the water, you can convert your spin-momentum back into the eddy as soon as you cross the eddy-line.

What strokes you take.

- Use the peel-out technique to get yourself established on the wave. After you're surfing, you can use a rudder to control the surf. If you try to use the rudder too soon (before crossing the eddy-line), it won't always work. It's critical to have the option of a power stroke as you enter the wave, which you have with the forward stroke that turns into a stern draw. Once you begin to use the rudder, you're actually forcing the boat downstream. If you start losing the bow, you'll have to rudder harder, and you'll pull yourself right off the wave.

Now you are there and ready to stay there. Have fun!

Boofing

It is hard to beat the feeling of a good boof stroke pulling your boat off the water.

Boofing is the act of lifting your bow over an obstacle. You can do a boof on a 12-inch drop or a 30-foot drop. You can also do it with the assistance of a rock, a wave, or a drop-off in the river. Boofing can be a very easy move or, given the wrong circumstances, a very difficult move. The type of boat you are in affects

A high-speed boof over a hole can be exhilarating.

the boof tremendously as well. The good news is that the main strokes and concepts for the boof are very consistent, making it fairly easy to learn.

Since this is a strokes and concepts book, I'll focus on the head, paddle, boat, and body movements you need to initiate and stick a good boof.

One of the main benefits of the boof for your river running is that you can stay in control on top of the water and carry your speed past the drop. A good example would be a 5-foot waterfall. You could run it by paddling up to the drop, letting the bow drop to vertical, plugging in and getting stopped by the hole, and then surfing the hole out; or you could simply paddle up to the drop, do a boof stroke, and land on top of the hole with downstream momentum that will carry you safely past the hole with no challenges. A good boof makes kayaking much easier on steeper rivers and anywhere there are holes to get over.

Keeping a boof stroke in the water even after you have left the drop helps keep the bow at the desired angle.

Head: Your head should spot your target, which is your "takeoff point." Once you get to the take-off point, your new target is the landing point.

Body: Keep your body weight over the boat, but let your body lean back about 20 degrees right before you do the boof stroke. Lift your knees up and bring your body back to neutral during the boof stroke to "lift the bow."

Boat: Drop some paddle-side edge with the boat to help slice the stern in the water and shorten the waterline. Angle the boat slightly to one side or the other. If there's a rock, angle your boat toward the rock by about 30 degrees to help you boof behind the rock and avoid the hole at the bottom. If there's no rock, then 10 to 20 degrees is enough to assure you get a good boof.

Paddle: Use medium-paced forward strokes up to the take-off point, reaching your boof stroke on or over the edge of the drop on the downstream side. If you are angled a little right, you should boof with a left stroke, as you have the space for it and it will be easier to reach over the drop. A boof stroke can be a simple, long, vertical, forward stroke, or it can be a sweeping forward stroke, or it can be a C-stroke. It's easiest to start with a long forward stroke. The key is the timing. If you stroke too early, your stroke will end before the drop, and your bow will just fall anyway. If you stroke too late, your bow will already be dropping, and you might not be able to reverse that momentum to keep the bow up.

THE MAIN CHALLENGES FOR THE BOOF

Your goal for the boof is to keep the bow from dropping down so far that it goes underwater on the landing. Keeping your bow up on a drop is about timing the stroke in such a way that you prevent the bow from dropping when it would normally start to drop (when your butt is getting up to the edge) by both doing a stroke that lifts the bow and by lifting the bow with your knees. If you do both of those things at the right time, you can keep your bow dry on most drops.

Reaching to the edge of the drop before taking the boof stroke gives you maximum stroke and best chance of success.

Stroke Timing: Most people who are learning to boof start and finish their boof stroke way too early. This is because they don't want to miss it, so they get excited and start the stroke when the bow is just getting to the drop instead of waiting until they can reach over the drop slightly.

Body Movement Timing: Remember that for every action, there is an equal and opposite reaction. Most people lean back right as they do the boof stroke. While leaning back for a boof does help, if you do it too late, it has the opposite effect. If you lean back right as you boat is going over the drop, you are essentially pushing your feet and bow down to vertical. If you want the bow to stay up, you need to lean back before you get to the edge, starting to pressurize your knees, and then the moment you take your boof stroke, lift hard on your knees to hold the bow up.

FLATWATER PRACTICE FOR THE BOOF

With a Friend: Paddle forward slowly, and when you almost get to your friend's boat, lean back 20 degrees and take a hard forward stroke, keeping your top hand back by your face and actually lifting the bow up with your forward stroke onto your friend's boat. You'll need to lift with your knees hard at the same moment as the stroke. If you are in a river running or creek boat, your bow might lift 12 inches, which is enough to get onto a kayak. If you are in a playboat, your bow might lift 24 inches—especially if you also drop some edge when you do the boof stroke.

Solo Practice: Find a downed tree branch or a rock that is only about 12 inches out of the water. Paddle toward it at half speed, and then boof your bow on top of it. Practice with some different edge drops to see how much edge works best for you in your boat.

Common Mistakes:
1. You don't lean back early enough (before you do the stroke), and you don't lift hard enough with your knees to get the bow up.
2. Your stroke is too early, and so your bow goes up and back down before it gets onto your friend's boat or the obstacle.
3. Your stroke is too late, so your bow doesn't have time to go up over the boat or obstacle before you hit it.

BOOFING OFF OF DIFFERENT TYPES OF ROCKS

Not all rocks are created equally. Some are smooth and easy to use for boofing, while others are grabby and not good for sliding over. Some are sharp, and some are rounded. Some are big and vertical and out of the water, and some are flat and just under the water, making a nice pad for boofing.

You need to adjust your approach based on the rock you are going to boof off. I'll give you the basic rules for the different types of rocks.

First, you don't have to get all the way up onto a dry rock to use it for boofing. Typically, the farther you get from the point where the water and the rock meet, the deeper the water is. Also, the closer you can get to a dry rock without getting slowed down too much, the easier it is to boof. For smooth granite rocks, it's good to actually get your boat on the dry rock, as your boat will slide smoothly over it, and you will land in the eddy behind the rock.

RULES FOR ROCKS

1. *Rough, grabby rocks*: Get as close to the rock as you can without hitting any of it (or at least not very much of it).
2. *Medium, semi-smooth rocks*: Get up to the rock and plan on having your boat touch the rock under the water, but not on the dry rock.
3. *Jagged rocks*: Get as close to the rock as you can without touching it—not even the wet rock under the water.

THE LATE BOOF

So far you've learned how to reach over the edge, which assumes there is a clear edge to the drop you are boofing. The more difficult boofs are when the drop "rolls" slowly downward. In these situations, you can't boof at the very top and still keep the bow up by the bottom. You'll need to do what is called a "late boof." The late boof is not as clean and obvious as types of boofs you've already learned. Instead of launching off the side of the rock and through the air, you just keep your bow up enough to avoid going under very far, and this allows you to carry your speed out from a drop, generally without going underwater.

All drops have a point where the water is at a 45-degree angle to the landing pool. This is generally when you should begin your late boof stroke, so you should treat this point as the "edge" of that drop. The type of boat you're paddling makes a difference, of course. A short playboat can late boof at the very bottom of any drop, while a longer boat's late boof should be much higher up the drop (because it is much harder to boof a long boat). Since we are talking about boofing, I will assume you are in a creek boat or a river runner that's 8 to 9 feet long. A boat this long should be late boofed at the 45-degree point.

Head: Look for your boofing zone (where the water is at a 45-degree angle to the landing) as you go over the horizon line.

Body: Keep your weight over the boat, leaning back slightly as you approach the drop.

Boat: Angle it slightly to either side. In a late boof, the best side for the

Long into this rolling drop, the boof shouldn't begin until the last good place for a stroke before the free fall.

boof stroke is on the upstream side. So if you want to do a left boof stroke, be angled left, and if you want to do a right boof stroke, be angled right. Edge your boat with the upstream edge in the water slightly (30 degrees). You can edge between 0 and 90 degrees, but while 90 degrees will show off your balance, anything more than 45 is unnecessary.

Paddle: As you crest the top of the drop, reach forward with your boof stroke and plant it in the water. Wait on the stroke, reaching far forward for the moment you hit the 45-degree point (boofing spot), and then pull your stroke hard and long, trying to keep that same stroke in the water until your boat lands at the bottom of the drop.

If you did it right, you will have lifted your bow up enough to keep it from diving. Your speed will carry out from the drop and you'll land with your stroke still pulling. This is a key skill for creek-boating where the holes are sticky and the drops are not vertical. It also helps on normal rivers where you want to boof over the bigger holes.

Boofing over Holes

Most people try to go around holes in the river, thinking that it is easier and safer. The reality is that the backwash of a hole slows your speed and is usually pretty stable water to sit on while negotiating a rapid. The lines around the holes are not necessarily easier and certainly don't allow you to take as much time in the rapid to set up your lines. If you are not comfortable boofing over holes, you are limiting your river-running and creeking abilities. Once you are comfortable, you'll find yourself boofing over some really big holes that you might not want to surf, but the line is easy and you are fine with it.

Head: Spot the take-off point on the horizon line of the hole.

Boat: Angle the boat to allow your boof stroke to straighten you out so that you land at the angle you want to hit the backwash. If you want to land 30 degrees to the left, angle 45 degrees to the left and do a big left boof stroke. If you want to land pointed straight downstream, angle 15 degrees to the left and use a left boof stroke. With experience, you'll be able to angle many different ways and use different boof strokes to change your angle on the landing. You can C-stroke for your boof stroke and actually be turning toward your paddle

Gnarly holes are tamed when you know you can keep your boat flying over them with a dependable boof.

stroke when boofing, or you can sweep boof to turn away from the paddle for the landing.

Body: Keep your body weight over the boat. You will see a lot of top boaters leaning *way* out to the side on boofs, often over 90 degrees. That is called a "lean boof." It is a trick boof that is just a style thing to do to look cool. It is fun. I like doing the lean boof, but it isn't necessary unless you just want a bigger challenge on the drops you are running. Remember to lift hard on your knees to keep the bow up . . . that is the boof part of the boof!

Paddle: Use any stroke that lifts the bow at the moment it would normally drop due to the water dropping away over the rock.

Landing a boof over a hole: Flatten the boat out, and remember that you are going very fast relative to the water. If you lean downstream at all, you will catch your edge. Treat the backwash like an eddy, and lean into it (upstream).

SUMMARY

It takes all kinds of strokes to get you and your whitewater kayak down a river, in and out of eddies, across the river for a ferry, boofing over a drop, S-turning through a mid-river eddy, and attaining up a drop. All of those strokes are spelled out here in this book. The drills are designed to be quick and easy to do as part of a physical warm-up or just as a learning experience. Taking the time to really get proficient with your strokes and understanding and applying the concepts is quite rewarding. You will be very happy with how your paddling takes a big step forward, and your friends will wonder what happened that you got so good, so fast!

I hope we get to paddle together on the river one day, if we haven't already. I have paddled over 11,000 times in a whitewater kayak for over thirty years. I have had the pleasure of paddling with many of you already, as well as many of

your parents, your kids, and your friends. Whitewater kayaking has been a passion, sport, hobby, business, and learning experience for me for most of my life. I hope you find that the information I am presenting to you is helpful in your own paddling.

Thank you for taking the time to absorb and pass on this information. The more people who understand kayaking's best practices, the more fun everyone will have!

See you on the river—EJ